To parents and teachers

We hope you and the children will enjoy reading this story in either English or French. The story is simple, but not *simplified,* so the language of the French and the English is quite natural but there is lots of repetition.

At the back of the book is a small picture dictionary with the key words and how to pronounce them. There is also a simple pronunciation guide to the whole story on the last page.

Here are a few suggestions on using the book:

- Read the story aloud in English first, to get to know it. Treat it like any other picture book: look at the pictures, talk about the story and the characters and so on.

- Then look at the picture dictionary and say the French names for the key words. Ask the children to repeat them. Concentrate on speaking the words out loud, rather than reading them.

- Go back and read the story again, this time in English *and* French. Don't worry if your pronunciation isn't quite correct. Just have fun trying it out. Check the guide at the back of the book, if necessary, but you'll soon pick up how to say the French words.

- When you think you and the children are ready, you can try reading the story in French only. Ask the children to say it with you. Only ask them to read it if they are keen to try. The spelling could be confusing and put them off.

- Above all encourage the children to have a go and give lots of praise. Little children are usually quite unselfconscious and this is excellent for building up confidence in a foreign language.

Published by b small publishing
Pinewood, 3a Coombe Ridings, Kingston-upon-Thames, Surrey KT2 7JT
© b small publishing, 1994
2 3 4 5
All rights reserved.
Design: *Lone Morton* Editorial: *Catherine Bruzzone* Production: *Grahame Griffiths*
Colour reproduction: *Vimnice International* Printed in Hong Kong by Wing King Tong Co. Ltd.
ISBN 1 874735 70 0 (hardback)
British Library Cataloguing in Publication Data. A catalogue record for this book is available from the British Library.

Goodnight everyone

Bonne nuit à tous

Lone Morton
Pictures by Jakki Wood
French by Marie-Thérèse Bougard

B SMALL PUBLISHING
BILINGUAL BOOKS

"Bedtime, Martha," called Mum.
"Yes Mum, we're nearly ready,"
replied Martha.

"Au lit, Marthe," dit Maman.
"Oui Maman, nous sommes presque
prêts," répondit Marthe.

"Monkey, you go there," said Martha,
"then you ... teddy,

"Toi, le petit singe, tu te mets là,"
dit Marthe,
"puis toi ... nounours,

and you two penguins,

et vous, les deux pingouins,

and you, baby rabbit.

et toi, petit lapin.

Mustn't forget you, big gorilla,
and you panda,

Je ne t'oublie pas, le gros gorille,
et toi le panda,

and rag doll Anna,

et Anna, ma petite poupée,

and you three...
mouse, lamb, and snake ...

et vous trois ...
la petite souris, l'agneau, et le serpent ...

and elephant.

et l'éléphant.

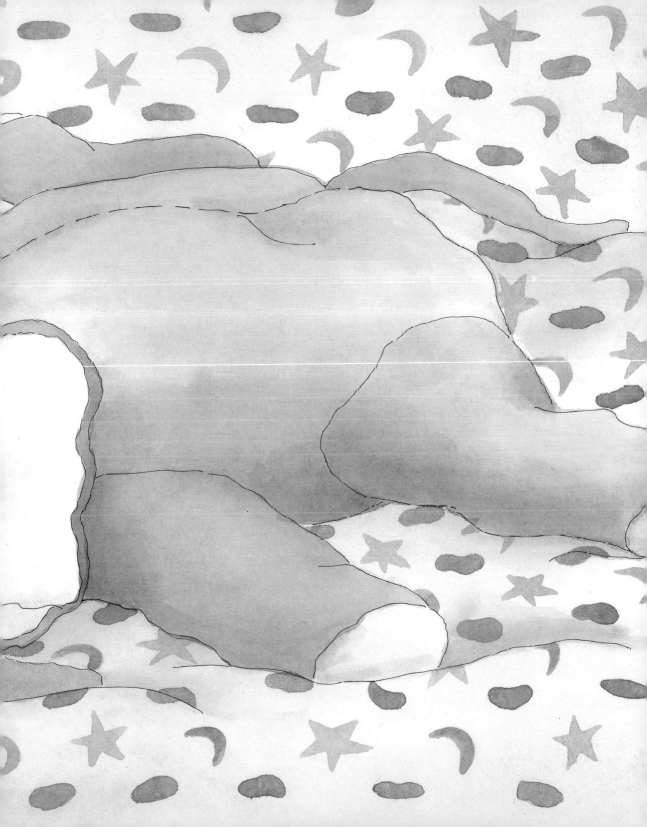

Oh, and I'll put my books here,
and my clock next to my pillow,
and my slippers by my bed."

Oh, et je mets mes livres ici,
et mon réveil à côté de mon oreiller,
et mes pantoufles à côté du lit."

"Are you ready yet?" asked Mum.
"Yes," said Martha.
"But where will *you* sleep, Martha?"

"Tu es prête maintenant?" demanda
Maman.
"Oui," dit Marthe.
"Mais toi, Marthe, où vas-tu dormir?"

"In bed with them.
Like this!" said Martha.

"Au lit, avec eux.
Comme ça!" dit Marthe.

"Well, goodnight Martha
and goodnight everyone," said Mum.

"Eh bien, bonne nuit, Marthe,
et bonne nuit à tous," dit Maman.

"Sweet dreams!"

"Faites de beaux rêves!"

Pronouncing French

Don't worry if your pronunciation isn't quite correct. The important thing is to be willing to try. The pronunciation guide here will help but it cannot be completely accurate:

- Read the guide as naturally as possible, as if it were British English of a generally South-Eastern variety (so-called RP).
- Put stress on the letters in *italics* e.g. lombool-*onss*.
- Don't roll the r at the end of the word, for example in the French word **le** (the): ler.

If you can, ask a French person to help and move on as soon as possible to speaking the words without the guide.

Words Les Mots

leh moh

monkey
le singe

ler sanjsh

teddy
le nounours

ler noo-*noorss*

penguin
le pingouin
ler pang-*wah*

panda
le panda
ler pon-*dah*

rabbit
le lupin
ler lap-*pah*

mouse
la souris
lah soo-*ree*

gorilla
le gorille
ler gor-*ee*

lamb
l'agneau
lan-*yo*

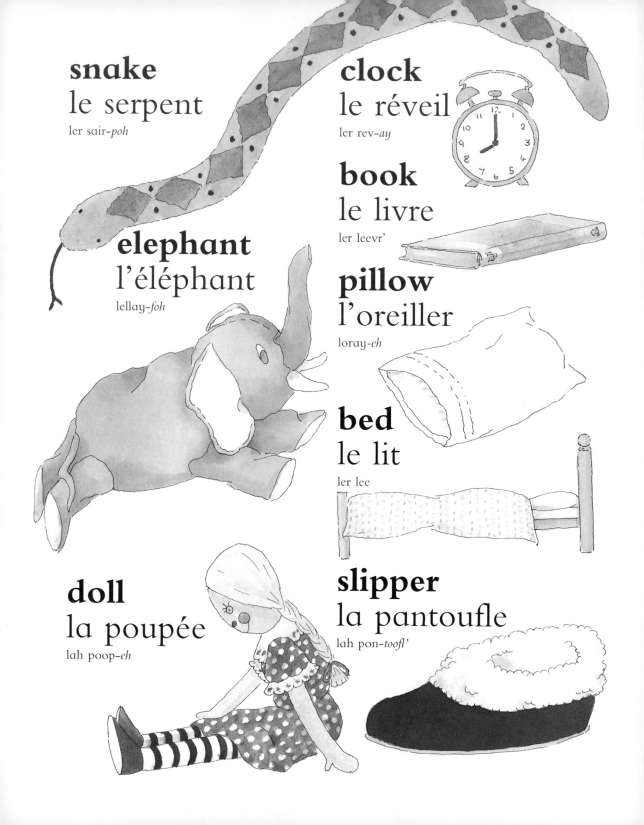

snake
le serpent
ler sair-*poh*

clock
le réveil
ler rev-*ay*

book
le livre
ler leevr'

elephant
l'éléphant
lellay-*foh*

pillow
l'oreiller
loray-*eh*

bed
le lit
ler lee

doll
la poupée
lah poop-*eh*

slipper
la pantoufle
lah pon-*toofl'*

A simple guide to pronouncing this French story

Bonne nuit à tous
bon nwee ah tooss

"Au lit, Marthe," dit Maman.
o lee, mart, dee ma-*moh*

"Oui, maman, nous sommes presque prêts," répondit Marthe.
wee mam*oh*, noo som presk preh, reh-pon-*dee* mart

"Toi, le petit singe, tu te mets là," dit Marthe,
twah, lcr p'tee sanjsh, too t' meh lah, dee mart

"puis toi ....,
pwee twah ... noo-*noorss*

et vous, les deux pingouins,
eh voo, leh der pang-*wah*

et toi, petit lapin.
eh twah, p'tee lap-*pah*

Je ne t'oublie pas, le gros gorille,
sh' n' too-*blee* pah, ler gro gor-*ee*

et toi le panda,
eh twah ler pon-*dah*

et Anna, ma petite poupée,
eh An-*na*, mah p'teet poop-*eh*

et vous trois …
eh voo trwah

la petite souris, l'agneau, et le serpent …
lah p'teet soo-*ree*, lan-*yo*, eh ler sair-*poh*

et l'éléphant.
eh lellay-*foh*

Oh, et je mets mes livres ici,
o, eh sh' meh meh leevr' ees-*see*

et mon réveil à côté de mon oreiller,
eh moh rev-*ay* ah cot-*eh* de moh oray-*eh*

et mes pantoufles à côté du lit."
eh meh pon-toofl' ah cot-*eh* doo lee

"Tu es prête maintenant?" demanda Maman.
too eh pret mat-*noh*? d'moh-*dah* ma-*moh*

"Oui," dit Marthe.
wee, dee mart

"Mais toi, Marthe, où vas-tu dormir?"
mch twah, mart, oo vah too dormeer?

"Au lit, avec eux."
o lee, avek er

"Comme ça!" dit Marthe.
com sah! dee mart

"Eh bien, bonne nuit, Marthe
eh bee-*yah*, bon nwee, mart

et bonne nuit à tous," dit Maman.
eh bon nwee ah tooss, dee ma-*moh*

"Faites de beaux rêves!"
fet der bow rev!